THE Journaling Genie™
IdeaBook

by melody ross

Table of Contents

The Story of
The Journaling Genie™

When I took the Genie designs off of the drawing table, I knew it would be a hot idea. I knew that I would use it all the time if I had it, but I am still in awe at the way that it all started, and how it has not let up a single bit. The Journaling Genie™ was destined to be a favorite tool for scrapbooking artists, and it has left everyone asking for more...

The Journaling Genie is one of those terrific, once in a lifetime ideas that has left many people thinking "why didn't I think of that?" That is precisely what I was thinking every time I took a ruler to my scrapbook pages and cards. Tired of waiting for someone else to design the product that I needed, I took it into my own, new company Chatterbox, Inc. and the Genie line gets more popular every day. To date, the Genies have won several awards and are in the hands of hundreds of thousands of scrapbooking artists worldwide. Wow!

The Journaling Genie made it's debut at the world famous Great American Scrapbook Convention '98 in Arlington, TX. I took 200 barely finished prototypes to the show to use in my classes and the frenzy began. When I announced to the eager scrapbookers that I could not sell them until all of my classes were over, I had no idea that I would walk out of my classroom to find hundreds of women waiting in a line that had formed an hour before my classes were through. And the rest is history......

The line of over 250 eager scrapbookers waiting for their chance to buy a Journaling Genie prototype stretched and winded through aisles at The Great American Scrapbook Convention in Arlington, TX. – May 1998

So What Is It?

A Journaling Genie™ is a highly functional, hugely fun and totally usable tool that you will wonder how you ever lived without. Made of heavy-duty, clear template material, it will last and last for all of your life's journaling adventures.

Space for fancy first letter!

Ideas printed right on the template!

Precision cut line guides to make perfectly straight, curvy, spiral, shaped... totally creative journaling!

Decorative edges to trace easy and jazzy borders to your pages!

Safe and easy storage in three ring binders!

#3 - FUNKY!

FANCY FIRST LETTER

THE Journaling Genie™

INSTRUCTIONS

START HERE & FOLLOW THE SWIRL FOR THE COOLEST WRITING EVER!

For more info. call CHATTERBOX INC.: (208)286-9517 or fax: (208)286-9828   © 1998 Melody Ross

...it's made for you!

How Does it Work?

The basic premise behind the Journaling Genie™ is a simple 3 step process. These steps will work for every Genie, and can be used by anyone at any skill level. More creative uses for the Genies are included in this book, but this is a very good place to start and you will be amazed at the other uses that are possible for your Genies...they are truly an unlimited resource! So let's go ahead and get started.....

STEP 1 Lightly trace around your selected Journaling Genie™ shape with a pencil on your choice of paper.

The Journaling Genie Idea Book ©

STEP 2

Remove the Journaling Genie™ and write lightly in pencil over the traced lines, to help prevent permanent mistakes.

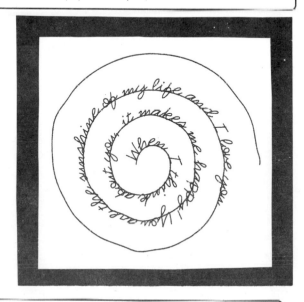

STEP 3

Trace over your words in ink and erase your pencil lines... a beautiful, timeless and easy Journaling Genie™ creation!

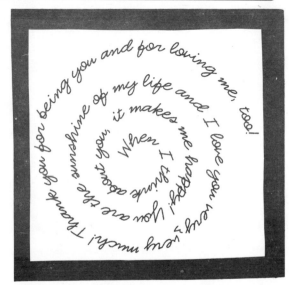

Tips for Success

USE A PENCIL!

Probably the most important companion tool to your Genie is a good pencil. Be sure to get yourself a hard lead pencil that can write very softly so that erasing the pencil lines is easy. I suggest that you also write your journaling out in pencil first, then go over it in ink, to prevent making permanent mistakes.

USE A GOOD ERASER!

There are so many kinds of erasers, and I have found that the kind of eraser that you use is also very important. Be sure to use a gentle eraser that will not scrape or scratch your paper. Use an eraser that doesn't leave too much residue, and does a clean job. I like simple white, retractable erasers.

WRITE LIGHTLY!

Avoid the urge to write with a lot of pressure. It is so much easier to erase and so much more attractive on your paper when there are no dents and "pencil stains" left behind where you traced the stencil. Just skim across the page and barely make a mark...just enough so that you can see it well.

USE A FLAT SURFACE!

Be sure to find a very flat, hard surface that is also large enough to hold your page and your Genie. If you have bumps and lumps and piles under your project, the pencil has a good chance of piercing your paper. If your surface is too soft, like a thick tablecloth, it will also pierce through your paper.

HOLD TIGHT TO YOUR GENIE!

With the opposite hand that you write with, hold your Genie tightly to your paper while you are tracing it. Be sure to hold it in the exact same place all the way along. This becomes kind of tricky when you are tracing one that has a lot of curves and angles...so be sure to hold on tight!

SPACE YOUR WORDS!

A lot of people ask me the best way to make all of the words fit properly in the shapes. I use hyphens sometimes, but usually, I just space words out a little more or a little less to make them fit just right.

REGULAR SPACING
A LITTLE MORE SPACED
A LITTLE LESS SPACED

What do I write?

- Write names, dates and places near your pictures
- Write your feelings about your pictures
- Write about smells, sounds, tastes and textures
- Write the words of your favorite songs
- Write things that your loved ones often say
- Write the words of your children's favorite rhymes
- Write your favorite quotes
- Write out your favorite jokes
- Write out your goals and dreams
- Write the current prices of the things that you buy
- Write about what's in the headlines
- Write about what makes you happy
- Write about the seasons
- Write directions to your house
- Write about your job
- Write a poem
- Write a letter to God
- Write all the things you wish you could say but never could...

> **NEED SOME BRAINSTORMING HELPERS?**
> Here's some terrific books to help you with the problem of knowing just what to write:
> - The Scrapbooker's Best Friend Vol. 1, 2 & 3 Hundreds of phrases categorized into sections in funny and heartwarming moods.
> - The Scrapbooker's Instant Interviews Over 600 thought-provoking questions to ask yourself, your parents, your children and anyone else that you love to capture vivid memories and thoughts.
>
> You can find out more about these books by looking in the Source Guide in the back of the book.

A few words about
Your Handwriting

Dear You,

This is a handwritten letter, just for you... I want you to read it as though you were the only person in the world reading it, because it *is* written just for you.

If you are like most people on earth, you probably do not like your handwriting, and this feeling keeps you from doing things that are so meaningful and important. Maybe you don't like to write, so you don't write notes to people that you love — maybe you are afraid that your handwriting will ruin your carefully laid-out scrapbooks & memory albums.

Think for a moment about your mother or father's handwriting.... if you were given a stack of essays, written by hundreds of different

...and Your Story

hands and you were told to choose the one that your mother or father wrote...you would actually be able to do it just based on the handwriting! Your children know yours, too! They affiliate your writing with you the same way they do your voice, your eyes. Your handwriting is as unique as your fingerprints are!

So in this day of computers, voice-mail and email, be sure to take some time to give the gift of yourself...whether it is to yourself or to someone else.

You may think that your life and your experiences are dull and ordinary... but you are a fascinating, unique individual...and people want to know all about you...in your words and in your handwriting. If you still don't like your handwriting...GET OVER IT! ☺

Sincerely,
Melody Ross - 1999

Creative Uses

Techniques for the Journaling Genie™ are only limited by your imagination! I have seen so many different, wonderful and creative uses by so many different artists! In this chapter, we will be discussing some of the best techniques for using the Genies that I have seen.

Let your mind wander as you see some of these terrific examples. Think to yourself about other ways that you might be able to use the Genies...perhaps we can publish some of your fresh ideas in the next idea book! Anytime you write a letter or any kind of journaling, think of ways that you might be able to incorporate the Genies into your creations.

The easiest and most inexpensive way to add variety to your Genie projects is to experiment with different colors of ink and paper! Write your words with lots of different colors, use lots of different kinds of paper!

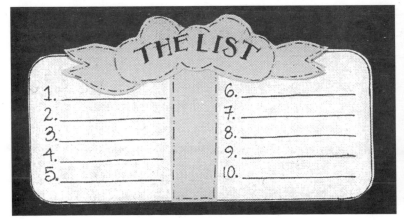

by Amber Hobbs

Dry embossing, layering & matting

Adding dimension to your journaling creations is one of the easiest and most effective techniques for utilizing the Journaling Genie collection.

The cut out lines on the Genies are perfect for embossing. Simply place the back side of your paper over the Genie, then use an embossing tool to rub the impression into your paper. Turn the paper over and you have a beautifully embossed work of art!

Layering and matting your Genie creations is something that I almost always do...experiment with different paper colors and textures. This adds so much beauty without very much effort!

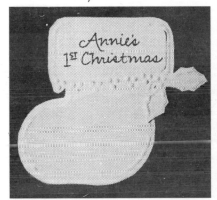

This embossed stocking has lace made from the holly berries & leaf on template #5

This tree has several different colors of layers backing it up adding a lot of dimension and texture to it.

This party hat was embossed at the edges, colored and layered with different colors.

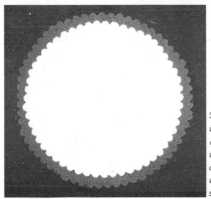

Simple white paper was used to trace the circle shape, then it was backed with colored paper and cut with decorative edge scissors.

Sections of the Genies can be used to emboss, as done in this sun made with one side of the rainbow on the Genie #3 FUNKY

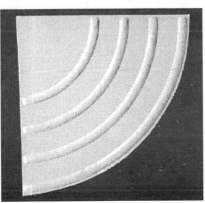

Creating "die-cut" shapes & paper-piecing

Journaling Genies™ are perfect for creating your own "die-cut" looking shapes. Simply trace along the edges and carefully make a clean cut with your scissors. You can also make some interesting styles by using decorative edge scissors. You'll see some incredible variations to the different shapes of Genies in the specific Genie sections. Try putting special details on your shapes after you have cut them out. You can create wonderful "die-cut" art by just adding a few special touches to your shapes.

Make a realistic looking cupcake using corrugated paper for the paper cup section. Cut out each section in a different color.

Use the swirl to cut a perfect shape for a swirly lollipop, cut the swirl out of a different color than the background, then glue a thin white strip for the sucker stick.

The top section of the stocking was cut on one end with decorative edge scissors, then the rest was cut out of a different color and glued together.

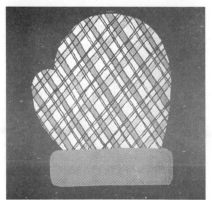

Use patterned paper for different parts of different shapes to make a custom look. This mitten was cut out of patterned paper, with a plain colored band out of a different piece, then glued together.

The shapes can be used in any direction, as shown here. The heart was cut out of red paper, backed with white, which was cut with decorative edge scissors, then the journaling lines were turned and placed right side up so that the writing on this shape would be nice & straight.

Tips for Success:

- Trace the shapes lightly in pencil so that after you have cut them out, you will be able to easily erase the pencil lines.
- The journaling lines on the Journaling Genies™ are perfect in many cases for separating the colors of paper that you will be using.
- If you are doing a lot of detailed cutting, try some smaller scissors so that you have more control.
- Use tweezers to help you place your work if you are working with a lot of small pieces.
- Use a safe glue with a small tip so that you can dab small amounts of glue into small places.
- Try using a craft blade if you need to clean up your cuts or slit on any of the lines.
- After your pieces are all glued together, try matting the whole piece with a complimenting color.
- Keep your options open with all of the creations that you make....use them in your scrapbooks, on cards to decorate notebooks, etc.

This terrific Easter basket was made with the oval shape and the weaving technique, then filled with punched grass and different colored eggs. The basket can be filled with anything you choose!

Use punches to decorate your shapes, like this hat was decorated with stars and a simple circle punch.

This heart goes a step further with punches to make a chocolate box full of little sweeties made with a circle punch and pens.

Using stamps, stickers & punch art

Stamping is such a beautiful art! Stickers and punches make an artist out of anyone! We have found that rubber stamps, stickers & punches are a perfect addition to the Journaling Genies. One of my favorite techniques is just to choose my favorite little itty bitty stamp, sticker or punch and just stamp or stick a border all the way around the Genie shape that I want to use. There are plenty of shapes and styles to choose from! Another technique is to draw the lines with the JG, then stamp your favorite image or stick your favorite sticker right in the middle of it and write all the way around it. Genies are perfect for making cards, too, just like rubber stamps, stickers and punches are!

Toy Stickers from The Gifted Line™ were placed around the oval of Journaling Genie #2 SHAPES

This elegant oval was made by randomly placing around maple leaf punches shapes*.

The circle shape was lightly traced, then beautiful ivy stamps by D.O.T.S. were stamped around the shape and colored for this very elegant bit of journaling using Journaling Genie #2 SHAPES

These adorable car punch shapes* were placed on a road made with the Journaling Genie #3 FUNKY

by Tracey Isidro

$\mathcal{H}$and doodling

Add a warm and heartmade touch to your page by hand-drawing borders and doodles on your pages. You can find all sorts of ideas from patterned paper and stickers. Find some that you like, then simply duplicate them in basic form as a border or a little doodle illustration. I love to try different borders around the shapes of my Genies. I will add a few ideas here, but do try lots of different styles for yourself.

Try this technique with any of the shapes. Just draw little doodles between the writing. If you are also using designer paper, look for patterns or doodles that you can copy to match your paper.

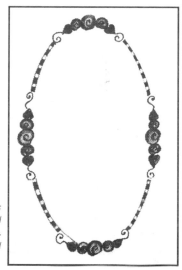

Make swirly little roses and checkers around the oval shape. The flowers fit well inside the bridge gaps of the shape. Trace in pencil first, then draw the border and erase the pencil lines.

Lightly trace the lines of the gift, then write words around the edges in different colors. Try this technique with any of the templates.

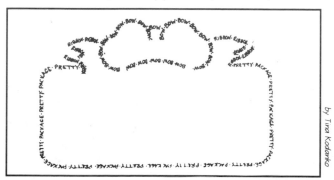

by Tina Kodanko

The circle shape was lightly traced, then a beautiful and surprisingly simple pine border was added. See The Scrapbooker's Book of Alphabets to learn the simple technique for this border in the alphabet called Pineneedles.

*W*eaving paper & making pockets

This technique is so incredible...and the great part is that it is also incredibly easy! Try this technique with any of the Journaling Genie™ styles, you will love it when people think that you just made something really intricate when it was really so simple!

You will need:

- *Your Journaling Genie™*
- *A craft blade knife (ie. X-acto™)*
- *A sharp pencil*
- *Scissors*

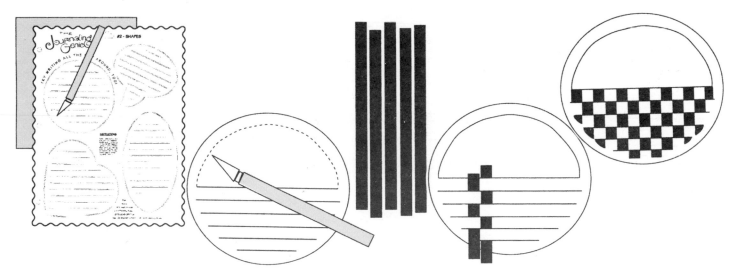

1. Trace around the outside of your chosen Journaling Genie™ with a pencil. Leave your Genie exactly where you traced and start cutting inside of the lines with your knife. Be sure to either keep your knife to the top of the open space or to the bottom of the open space on all of the lines. Cut all of the lines that you need to cut for the style that you have chosen.

2. Take the Journaling Genie™ off of your paper and cut around the traced edges until you have a cleanly cut shape.

3. Place the Journaling Genie™ on the color of paper that you are going to weave through the first color and cut through (with knife) all of the lines of the same shape. Cut the ends off with scissors so that you have strips.

4. Take the right length of paper strip and weave back and forth through the cut Journaling Genie™ shape. Weave through the opposite slits with the next paper strip and repeat.

5. Trim the paper strips to the right length and carefully glue down the ends with a tiny dab of glue.

Cutting pockets into your shapes:

There are a few ways to use this technique, and the supplies that you need are the same ones that you need for the weaving technique.

full pocket

You will need 2 different cut out shapes for this one. Once you have your selected shapes cut out, choose the one that will go on the top...this is the one that you will cut the pocket slit into. Simply lay the shape directly under the Journaling Genie™ that you used to make the shape, and cut a slit with a knife in the spot where you want the pocket to open. A pocket near the top of the shape will be best. Now, either glue on the very edges of the two shapes to attach them together or staple them around the edges.

slip pocket

This technique is almost exactly the same, but a little easier. Two slits will be cut this time to slip whatever you are wanting to slip through to the back and then back through to the front. Simply cut out your shape and then use the Journaling Genie™ lines to use as a guide to cut your slits with a knife. If you want your slits to go in a different direction than they are on the shape, just turn your Genie slightly to the direction that you want your slits to go.

What can I put into a pocket?

- Slip in movie or concert tickets...a perfect gift for anyone
- Put in clues for a scavenger hunt
- Stuff a stick of gum in a note in your child's lunch box
- Slip a receipt through for your album to show how much groceries cost in "our day"
- Put a special recipe in one along with a baked treat for your neighbor
- Slip a bubble-gum cigar in one for a baby announcement
- Make fortune cookies by slipping a "fortune" into the shapes for a fun party favor
- Fill one with real or chocolate coins for a fun gift to give to a child

Basic & Beautiful

Layout Ideas for JG #1 - BASIC

Spacing your lines

Don't feel like you are limited to the line spacing that is on the templates. If you skip a line or two, your writing can be as big as you want it to be. For titles and headlines, it is a good idea to skip a line or two and use the two lines as a guide for the top of your writing and the bottom of your writing. The journaling widths on the template are also varied, you can choose to do a long, skinny bit of journaling, or spread the journaling across the page.

CHRISTMAS

Jason

I remember that day like it was yesterday

The fancy first letter

This is another one of my favorite techniques, it is also a very popular technique in graphic design, you will see it used a lot in book layouts and magazine articles. You will see that there is a space left on the template just for this purpose. The reason that I like this technique so much is because I love to do decorative lettering, but it take so much time to do an entire word or title. The fancy first letter technique is great because you only have to write the first letter in a fancy alphabet. You can get as intricate and artistic as you want to...and you only have to do it once!

Making albums for my family is so rewarding! My favorite part is

Write your headline all the way down the side of your lines, then journal around it...a super easy, super great look for writing just about anything!

Write part of your title at the beginning of the journaling lines and the rest of the title at the end, then journal around them. This is a terrific look that anyone can do and it adds a wonderful touch to anything written.

Draw little shapes all around the journaling to match a shape that you draw around the fancy first letter.

Use the little title blocks at the bottom of the template for writing names and titles of anything. Write one letter in each block using your own handwriting, rubber stamps, or alphabet stickers. These titles were designed, created and decorated by punching expert Tracey Isidro, author of "Punch Happy"... with what else? PUNCHES!

by Tracey Isidro

other uses:

- Use the lines to make perfect stripes for backgrounds
- Turn the lines the other direction over stripes to make perfect checks and plaids
- Weave strips cut with the lines to make a paper baby quilt or picnic blanket
- Make the fancy first letter on a separate piece of paper, then cut it out and glue it in the fancy first letter space
- Trace a shape around the fancy first letter using shape template

Shaping Up

Layout Ideas for JG #2 -SHAPES

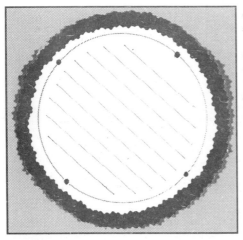

Customize any of the shapes by tracing around them and adding small doodles in the bridge holes, as done in this circle shape. Back with plain or patterned paper cut with fancy scissors.

A few simple techniques combined were used to make this terrific sunshine. The fancy first letter was cut from a different piece, words were written all the way around and the whole piece was matted with a different color.

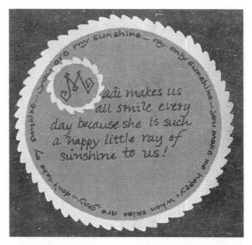

This weaved basket was filled with different colors and shapes of flower punches. Use the weaving technique, being sure to cut the handle out with scissors instead of a knife. Try filling the basket with other shapes, too.

The same weaving technique was used for this wonderful little pie. Corrugated paper was used as the base to add even more texture, and once the pie was completed and glued, a piece was cut and little circle punch cherries were added, along with a "crust".

A Chance Meeting...

the poem

Jennifer told Matt that he'd better come-up with something really creative if he wanted her to say yes to a marriage proposal...

Matt took on the challenge & made an event of it. He took Jen into the mtns, had a poem & a song & a picnic just waiting... and it worked!

#2 SHAPES

This page has all of the elements of an award winner! Careful and creative journaling tells the story behind the pictures, memorabilia adds texture and excitement, and paper weaving adds an artistic touch.

The heart shape was used for the journaling, as well as to make this wonderful memorabilia pocket. The front piece of the pocket was weaved with complimenting colors and stapled to a piece of cardstock that was cut just outside the traced line of the heart with decorative edge scissors. The top and bottom edges were traced on the long edge of the Genie with a white opaque pen.

This technique can be used for any occasion with any of the Genie shapes to customize a very special scrapbook page.

Perfect Pages

The rose on this page was created with the spiral of #3 FUNKY JOURNALING GENIE. The beautiful edges were created by tracing the wavy lines of the same template. Hand made roses were created to compliment the very creative journaling piece to add a very lovely touch to this priceless scrapbook page. Memorabilia was included with the handwritten memory to make a personalized momento that will last forever.

page by Zelphie Winegar

Idaho City
City Hall
1998

KELLY &
SHERILYN

This very creative & fun page utilizes the swirl shape of the Journaling Genie #3 FUNKY. An adorable lollipop and a cute little snail are perfect for the sentiments that were written around the swirl shape. Little punched shapes were placed through the rest of the page to create an artistic touch to this terrific page.

Notice that the journaling on this page is as full of impact as the beautiful pictures. Another handcrafted work of art that is as original as the face in the pictures. The sunshine was created using paper and The Journaling Genie #3 FUNKY.

TWO YEARS OLD!!

FISCHER · JEREMY · JACOB · LAUREN

Blow
the candles,
Wish away.
You are the
superstar
of the
day!

LAUREN · FISCHER · JACOB · AND · DYLAN

This is a perfect example of what can be done with simple paper and ink. This page was created using different colors of ink and templates. This page looks like designer paper, but is a handcrafted original work of art.

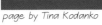

This very stylish page was created by tracing the spiral shape in pencil, then turning the template around and tracing the spiral again with the back of the template on the facing page. The design between is a simple freehand in pencil. Once the design was complete, journaling was written all the way from the beginning to the end. Titles were placed on either side with *Journaling Genie #1 BASIC*.

The creativity for the journaling on this page required only ink and *The Journaling Genie #3 FUNKY*. The Genie was placed directly on the page where it should go, then the shapes were traced in ink to not only add the lettering guide line, but also a decorative, colorful touch. The colorful lines were then journaled on and a perfect page was done!

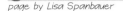

page by Lisa Spanbauer

This whimsical page was created by tracing out the spiral on the purple paper, then cutting it out entirely with a knife or fine scissors. The purple page was then placed on top of the yellow page and the journaling was written in the cutout...cool!

A blank page is a perfect gift for a baby shower, a wedding shower, graduation, birthday or any other special occassion. Simply write basic details that should be included about the event, then leave space for the recipient to journalize with their personal experiences. Leave spots for pictures with photo corners, making it a user-friendly page. This one was made by using *Journaling Genie #6 BABY*.

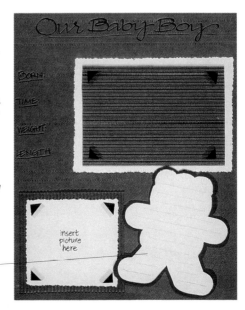

The oval shape on **Journaling Genie #2 SHAPES** was used to create these adorable grandparents and also the journaling piece. The ends were cut off of the oval piece to make the barrel shape.

Dry embossing the edges of any Genie shape is a very nice touch to use on elegant pages. A fancy first letter on a separate piece of paper was made, then glued to the matted shape.

Stickers were placed in the "bridge" areas of the circle shape on #2 SHAPES to make this simple, yet great looking title page. This method is great for any page! The perfect phrase written around the edge was found in The Scrapbooker's Best Friend book.

page by Shelly Smitheram

Page by Zelphie Winegar

The journaling on these pages was completed with the wavy sections of **Journaling Genie #3 FUNKY** and it was so easy! The Genie lines were traced directly on to the page, then journaling was written over it. The border was also made by writing wavy phrases all the way around. Once the ink was dry, the pencil lines were erased...and voile!...a terrific looking page!

Simple strips of paper were used to make arms and glued to the mittens on this adorable page done with the **Journaling Genie #5 CHRISTMAS**, paper and punches. A simple, beautiful, designer look.

The rainbow shape found on **Journaling Genie #3 FUNKY** makes terrific titles for pages when used with a title strip. Try using this shape both by itself and turned upside down as seen on this simple page layout.

This is the perfect technique for writing about a really special event in your life or for making a poster or writing a letter with a few pictures added. Simply lay down your pictures and decorations, then take your #1 BASIC *Journaling Genie* and draw very light pencil lines across the places where there are not any pictures... then journal on the lines and erase the pencil lines!

Notice how the Genies were used both directly on the page and as a glued-on cut out shape

This adorable blanket was easily created using the Paper Weaving technique, slitting every other line on **Journaling Genie #1 BASIC** and weaving paper strips between each slit. The blanket was then simply trimmed with accenting color paper strips and a pretty edge was made with decorative edge scissors.

Matte pictures with Genie shapes and create drama by overlapping shapes with other colors as seen on this tree shape made with the **#5 CHRISTMAS Journaling Genie**

page by Zelphie Winegar

page by Lisa Spanbauer

Write your favorite joke inside of the quotation bubble, then write laughter all the way around it.

Use this technique in a variety of different ways. Try the faces of friends, with real pictures. Put several different pictures of the same person in the chocolate box too, and write something like..."The Many Flavors of Johnny" ...Just get creative!

Turn the quotation bubble upside down to make the cutest little boy ever! This boy resembles "Alfalfa" from The Little Rascals, but we all know a little boy with a defined cowlick!

Use this adorable "back of a baby" profile to journal some very cute sentiments about a baby in your life. This one was made with both the heart shape (as the bottom) and the circle shape (as the head). Ears were made with a circle punch and the little hair was cut free-hand. The diaper was cut out of a white sheet with the point cropped off to expose the back of the baby.

Draw a simple ivy border around the heart, and add little swirl rosebuds and leaves.

Make a sweet little butterfly by using two of the heart shapes and free-handing the body. This one was cut with fancy scissors and journaling was written on both of the wings.

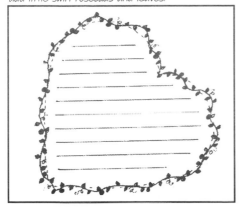

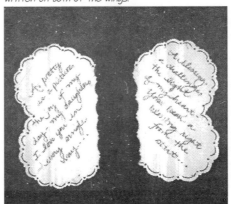

The ovals are perfect for making a whole cast of characters. These grandparents were made using circle punches as ears and glasses and free-hand the other little touches. Try some of the other ideas for for people on the next page.

Cut the oval in half to make this sensational snow globe. Don't be limited to using a snowman inside, try any shape you want to...even a real photograph of someone you know, covered with transparent vellum!

Hand-draw a pretty border around the oval, with lots of dots and a few little flowers placed in the bridge gaps.

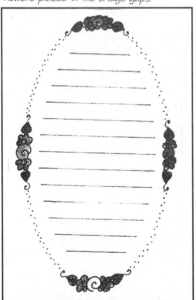

A universal sentiment! Make this humorous lady using hair strips cut with zig-zaggy scissors and glued to her head.

Use your favorite little punch shapes or stickers to make a really great journaling piece, like this one cut with fancy scissors.

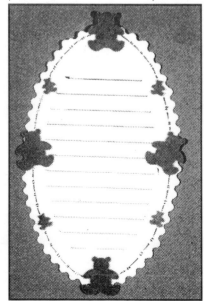

22

more ideas:

Getting Funky

Layout Ideas for
JG #3 - FUNKY

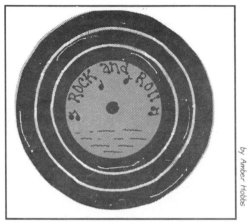

by Amber Hobbs

This little record album can be used for so many things! Try writing your favorite little musician's name on the title. This was made with the rainbow, right side up...then upside down!

This is another piece made by turning the rainbow upside down after tracing it right side up. Use little shapes inside the center line and write around the top and bottom of them. Use a title strip for the middle cut from a different color.

Follow the lines perfectly to make the layers of a watermelon slice. Make the bottom layer in green, the middle layer in white and the center layer in red, cutting a nice bite out of the red section and drawing in seeds. A little bit of journaling will fit perfectly inside of the white layer.

The rainbow also works perfectly to create citrus fruit slices. Try: oranges, lemons & limes.

And we can't forget the simple rainbow! Use colored pencils or chalks to lightly color the different colors of the rainbow, then journal over the colors with a dark ink!

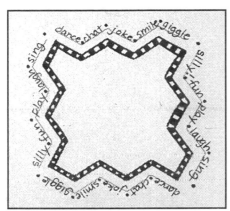

Use the jaggedy lines to make this terrific word frame for a special picture. Simply draw one line on each side, then journal above each line. Fill in the frame with checkers for an simple added touch.

The journaling inside of this bottle was created with the small wavy lines. Try combining the Genies for different looks like this one. Almost any of the shapes can be journaled inside of with wavy or jaggedy lines from the #3 FUNKY template.

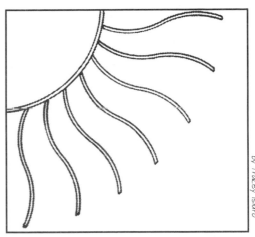

by Tracey Isidro

For an artsy looking sunshine, draw the corner of the circle and draw rays shooting out with the small wavy lines. Try journaling on each little ray.

This great little boot track was made by tracing the big line of the rainbow for the top and the upside down little line of the rainbow for the heel. The shape was completed around the lines, then filled in with the jaggedy lines for the boot tread.

This great little flag was made by filling in the little wavy lines with red marker to make stripes. Try journaling not only on the very top, but also in each white stripe... the perfect bit of journaling for patriotic projects!

by Tina Kodanko

This is another sunshiny idea, this time using the swirl shape. Notice that only part of the swirl is used. A triangle shape was added all the way around to make funky little sun rays and the journaling is just right!

by Kallie Wilkins

Once again, only part of the swirl is used on this terrific word frame. Draw the swirl in pencil and place a small matted picture inside of it...then journal all the way around on the remaining swirl shape...totally cool!

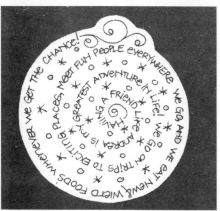

This is a terrific look using just ink and paper and your trusty Genie! Add little doodles in between your words to make a crafty and artsy little bit of journaling for any project!

You can see another variation of this lovely rose on the first page of the color examples at the center of the book. The color is entirely up to you...just be sure add your journaling in a color that will show-up!

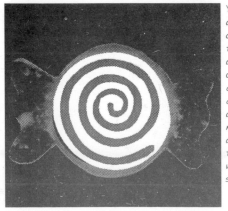

You can either make a peppermint candy or a lollipop by cutting out the swirl and mounting to a different colored circle. The wrapper can be made out of any transparent material. We cut apart a page protector to make the wrapper for this sweet treat.

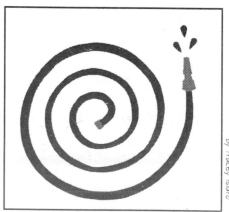

A bit of precision cutting made this great little hose. Simply trace the swirl shape on both edges, and cut it out of green or black and then add a nozzle out of yellow paper and some blue water drips.

by Tracey Isidro

The wavy lines are perfect for making a road shape. Try journaling on the road, adding little landmarks that you have in your area or a trip that you went on, or taking a small picture of your own vehicles and adding that to the road.

The wavy lines are also perfect for making a fun musical scale. Use musical note stamps or stickers to add even more flair. Write the words to a favorite song...one of your own or your child's. Write the words to the jingle of one of your favorite products or a commercial that is on television all the time.

making waves:

The Wavy lines are perfect for borders & designs!

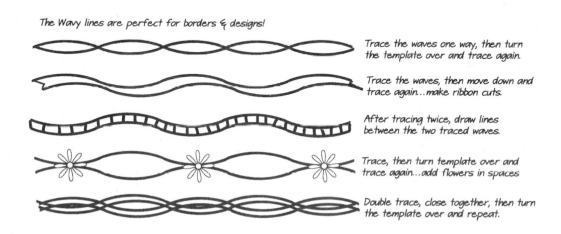

Trace the waves one way, then turn the template over and trace again.

Trace the waves, then move down and trace again...make ribbon cuts.

After tracing twice, draw lines between the two traced waves.

Trace, then turn template over and trace again...add flowers in spaces

Double trace, close together, then turn the template over and repeat.

Let's Party!

Layout Ideas for JG #4 - BIRTHDAY

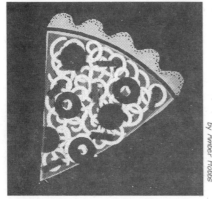

by Amber Hobbs

Use the party hat to make a yummy slice of pizza and decorate with different punches and paper scraps.

by Shelly Smitheram

The party hat can also be used to make a pretty dress on a paper doll. Add lots of little touches with other punched shapes.

This princess hat is as easy as can be... just cut off the bottom frills and add a scarf to the back.

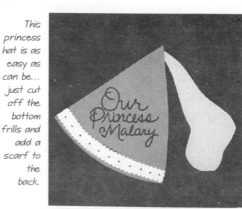

by Amber Hobbs

A lovely greeting card can be made with any of the Journaling Genie shapes, this one was made by layering the party hat and the noisemaker, which were decorated with punched shapes and markers.

To make this tempting slice of pie, simply slit each line with a knife, and slip little red punched circles to resemble cherries...try other flavors, too!

by Amber Hobbs

Embossing the hat is a very nice touch. This one was colored lightly with colored pencils, but the same technique could be used with chalks. The journaling was written with a white opaque pen.

This sweetie was made with the balloon shape. The ears could have been made with the ends of the balloon, but these were made with a circle punch. The pacifier also used a circle punch and the handle is a cutout heart. The hair was made by folding a daisy punch in half.

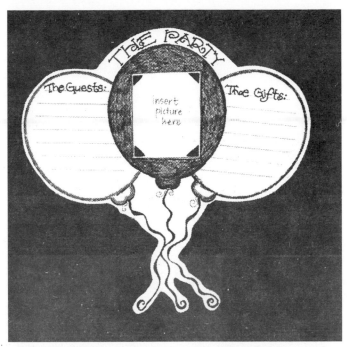

These three balloons make a great page layout. Blank page layouts such as this can also be given as a very thoughtful and useful gift.

A hose can be made from the noisemaker shape by simply adding a nozzle. Add some grass and a puddle for even more impact. There is plenty of space on the hose to write a title or a small bit of journaling.

This goofy and fun bug was made with the balloon turned sideways with the end cut off. The antennas were traced and cut from the noisemaker shape. Add some big bug eyes made from a circle punch.

Another adorable little guy made with the balloon shape turned sideways. The baker hat is made with the cupcake turned upside-down. This hat was cut out of wavy corrugated paper by DMD™. The glasses are a circle punch.

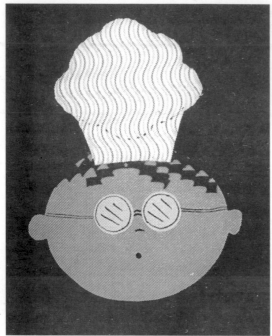

Create your own custom design by tracing a shape and coloring it in with whatever colors you choose, like this cute cupcake colored and shaded with colored pencils.

The bow and the ribbon are cut from a different color of paper than the gift body. Separate the lines of the present with a strip of paper to represent a ribbon. The two rows of lines are perfect for writing a gift list...ask a child what he or she wants for Christmas or a birthday...or write your own list!

The top of the cupcake makes a perfect ice cream scoop! Follow the side lines of the cup and make a triangle for the cone.

Use a circle punch to make an adorable baby face to announce to arrival of the most precious gift! You can also use this idea and put actual pictures and slit an opening to slide the pictures partially in. Don't limit the faces to baby faces, either! A friend or loved one is also one of life's greatest gifts!

Look what you can do when you turn the cupcake upside down! This adorable Santa was made with just 3 colors of paper and lots of creativity! Use this Santa on any Christmas project along with a journaling shape from the Christmas Genie.

by Lisa Spankauer

Another really cute ice cream cone idea made with the cupcake. Add a dollop of whipped cream with white paper and draw on sprinkles or use paper confetti. Finally, put the cherry on top with a circle punched from red paper.

by Amber Hobbs

All that you need for this terrific little work of art is white paper and ink. After you trace the shape, just color it in your choice of colors, shading the sides and journal down the middle!

With a few star stamps and some paper backing, this balloon has dimension and texture that makes all the difference! The string can either be drawn on with a white pen or you can glue on real string.

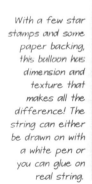

Slip just about anything in this great little gift pocket. See the section on paper weaving and pocket making to learn about this cool technique.

Turn the top of the cupcake right side up, then turn it upside down to make perfect little clouds for any occasion.

by Amber Hobbs

Christmas

Layout Ideas for JG #5 CHRISTMAS

This simple and lovely little tree was traced on white paper, then chalked around the edges in the appropriate colors and journaled on the penciled journaling lines. Once it was complete, it was matted in a complimenting color.

by Shelly Santheram

Use any of the Genie shapes to decorate a gift bag. This tree shape was journaled on a diagonal to look like garland. The corrugated gift bag is from DMD™.

This tree is double matted and placed on a matted frame. The different colors and layers add a very nice touch to this bit of journaling that will be one of the highlights of the page.

The dress on this darling little girl was made from the tree turned upside down. If you look closely, the head and hair of the little girl are made from the reindeer head.

by Lisa Spanbauer

A real candycane could take the place of this paper one that is slipped between two slits cut into the tree. See more about this technique in the weaving & pocket section.

The top layer of this tree was cut from white paper and cut in a wave to resemble snow on the top of the tree. The white section was a perfect spot for journaling.

by Lisa Spanbauer

This terrific rocket is the tree with the bottom two layers of branches cut straight down. The fire out the back is made from a swirl punch.

by Amber Hobos

Who could resist this adorable hand puppet made from the mitten shape? Try lots of different faces and hair for this idea!

Weaving the mitten makes a really nice touch for any project. Try making a pair!

This mitten was decorated so wonderfully with punches and paper strips cut with fancy scissors. A great little bit of winter journaling.

by Cindy Barr

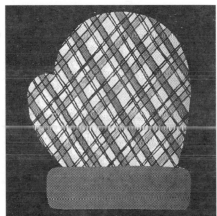

It's as easy as can be to make a great looking little mitten with just two colors of paper, one for the mitten and one for the band.

caption ideas:

- Home is the Heart of Christmas
- Christmas Glows With Love
- Family & Friends are the True Gifts of Christmas
- A Season with a Precious Reason
- All Hearts Come Home for Christmas
- Reindeer Crossing

- We Believe in Santa Claus!
- Have a Jolly Jolly Christmas
- Warm Holiday Fun
- Come & See…the Christmas Tree!
- He's making a list…
- Wise Men Seek Him Still

All phrases found in *The Scrapbooker's Best Friend*

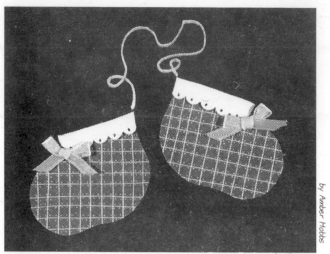

by Amber Hobbs

Trace out a stocking on the paper of your choice, then turn the template over and trace it again the other direction. Cut the tops off of the stockings to make sweet little baby booties.

Make a sock or a pair of socks by cutting the stocking out of white paper, trimming the top band section so that it is straight with the lower sides of each stocking.

Don't underestimate simple! This stocking is just cut from two different colors of paper and glued together. Small, easy touches are added by writing words around the edges.

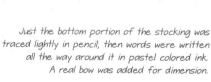

Just the bottom portion of the stocking was traced lightly in pencil, then words were written all the way around it in pastel colored ink. A real bow was added for dimension.

This stocking is very elegant looking, done in all white with embossing. The lacy edges are made by embossing the holly berries found at the bottom of the template. The leaves are also find at the bottom and were embossed, cut out and glued to the stocking shape.

by Tina Kodanko

34

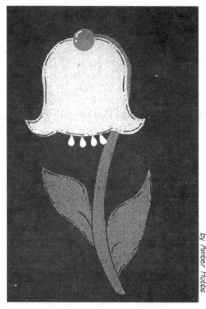

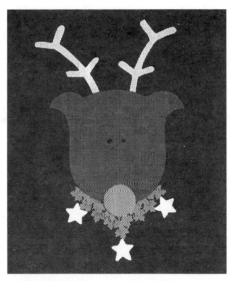

The details on this reindeer were made with colored pencils. This is a very charming, yet very inexpensive way to add an artistic touch to any winter time project.

Just cut the reindeer head (minus the ears and nose) out of blue paper and make a stem for this lovely bluebell flower.

Each piece of the reindeer was cut from the right color and then the pieces were glued together for this wonderful bit of paper art. The wreath around this deer's neck was made with leaf punch shapes cut from green paper.

This cute little girl was made by turning the reindeer head upside down and decorating accordingly. Try this with a dress made from the upside down christmas tree or party hat...absolutely adorable!

The Wedding or Christmas bells are ringing with this clever idea using the reindeer heads turned upside down. Make a whole arrangement of bells ringing...decorate some and journal on the others!

Oh Baby!

Layout Ideas for JG #6 BABY

Just make a circle to mount these itty bitty little feet onto, then glue them on and journal! To make the feet face opposite directions, first trace from the front of the template, then from the back.

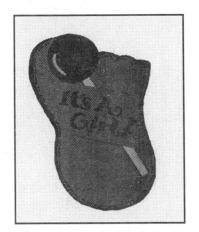

Slit a pocket into the little foot and slip in a treat to announce the birth of a child!

Simply trace the foot onto white paper, cut it out, turn it upside down, add a little face....and, BOO!

by Amber Hobbs

Cut out the carriage, using your choice of colors and paper, then cut a silhouette of a baby picture to place inside the carriage. Be sure to include the name of the baby!

This wonderful design includes two of the Genie styles. The baby was created with a circle punch and a few hand-drawn details. Try making a whole carriage full of babies!

The inside journaling of this bottle was made with the little wavy lines of the Genie #3. Punch decorations are a great touch.

To make a card out of any of the Genie styles, just fold a paper, trace the shape onto it with one side on the fold, then cut it out except for the fold.

by Amber Hobbs

This clipboard was made with the body of the bottle, the clip is the nipple turned upside down with a hole punched in it. Try journaling on this clipboard about doctor visits, immunizations, surgery, sports games, coaching, business....etc. etc. etc.

by Amber Hobbs

By simply leaving off the nipple of the bottle, you can create any kind of jar you might ever need! I'm sure you can think of a jar for every occasion, and the label is the perfect place for journaling!

The stamp pad on this idea was made with the body of the baby bottle, the stamp and the handle were made with the bottle ring. You can customize this for any occassion, too...use your imagination!

by Amber Hobbs

Make this funny lady's behind by turning the carriage upside down and cutting straight down the sides. Add ooh-la-las and socks.

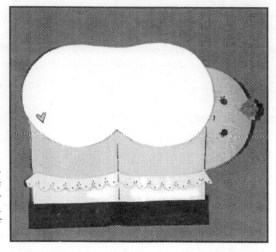

Using the same technique, make this precious litte baby bottom. To add the head, use the wheel of the carriage as a guide.

by Amber Hobbs

- "I'm a little behind in my scrapbooking"
- "I'm a little behind in my gardening"
- "I'm a little behind in my housework"
- "I'm a little behind in my potty-training"
- "I'm a little behind!"
- "Behind every great kid is a great mom"
- "Just bummin' around"
- "I'm bummed out!"
- "Let's get to the bottom of this"
- "I've bottomed out"

Think of all of the ways that you might be able to use a slice of bread...for journaling or for decorating! Make a scrapbook page about what kind of sandwich everyone in your family likes to eat...wouldn't that be fun to read in 20 years! Try this one with a jar of jam or peanut butter made with the baby bottle shape...ah, the possibilities are endless!

by Amber Hobbs

Decorate the outside of a scrapbook or journal with any of the Genie designs. This one also uses the title blocks found on #1 BASIC. The journaling on the inside of the scrapbook is all done with the teddy bear to match the front.

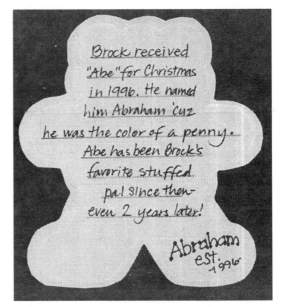

As you can see, the teddy bear looks absolutely adorable when used for simple scrapbook journaling. Make a whole family of bears, decorate some & journal on the others.

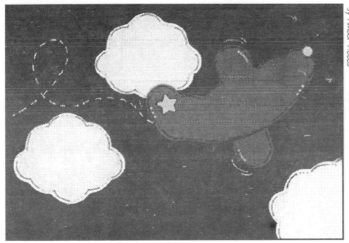

by Amber Hobbs

You have to look twice to see that this extremely clever airplane was made by cutting the bear down the middle and placing it on it's side. To make the other wing, cut an extra arm and glue to the sides. The perfect little clouds were made from the top of the cupcakes. #4-PARTY.

by Amber Hobbs

Make this cute bunny by turning the bear shape upside down and cutting off the head and midsection. The legs become the ears of the bunny. Decorate the cute little bunny with punched shapes.

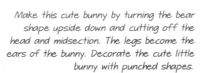

Source Guide

Paper:
Creative Memories
800.468.9335

Close To My Heart/D.O.T.S.
888.655.6552

Design Originals
800.877.7820

Hot Off the Press
503.266.9102

The Paper Patch
801.253.3018

Scissors & Punches:
Fiskars, Inc.
800.950.0230

Family Treasures
800.413.2645

Marvy-Uchida
800.541.5877

McGill, Inc.
815.568.7244

Stamps:
Close To My Heart/D.O.T.S.
888.655.6552

Inkadinkado Rubber Stamps:
781.938.6100

Personal Stamp Exchange
707.588.8058

Stickers:
Mrs. Grossman's Paper Co.
800.457.4570

Stickopotamus
201.939.5404

The Gifted Line
800.544.3833

Title & Phrase Books:
Chatterbox, Inc.
888.272.3010

About the Author:

Melody Ross is known as "The Journaling Queen" because of her enthusiastic passion for keeping journals and scrapbooks. Melody is also the wife of an adrenaline seeker, the mother of 3 beautiful children and the President of her own company, Chatterbox, Inc. Melody is the author of 6 other books and the creator and inventor of The Journaling Genie™ and the entire creative journaling template concept. Melody is an Idaho native and plans on spending her life where she grew up, near the mountains.

We ♥ Scrapbookers!™

This book was made especially for scrapbookers, by scrapbookers! Many of the wonderful ideas in this book using Journaling Genies were ideas by local scrapbookers in our area. We would like to thank them for their help and ideas and introduce them to you!

Cindy Barr, ID
Amber Hobbs, ID
Tina Kodanko, ID
Shelly Smitheram, ID
Lisa Spanbauer, ID
Kallie Wilkins, ID
Zelphie Winegar, ID

...and a very special thank you to Tracey Isidro, author of *Punch Happy-Punch Art Secrets for Scrapbooks and Gifts*. Some of Tracey's terrific ideas using punches with Journaling Genies are found in this book. To order Tracey's book, contact:
Living Vision Press
P.O. Box 326
Bountiful, UT 84011
801-292-6007